365 Happines

This collection of 365 quotes, based on appreciating life's pleasures and finding happiness. A combination of Happiness quotes that you can use better yourself and your mindset and set yourself up for massive amounts of Empower Encourage Happiness Success Motivation in your life . You should hopefully have a good understanding of how to utilize affirmation for the best result. You can pick and choose which of these you like the most, but try not to quickly read through all of these ones after another, unless that is how you like to do it and works best for you.Change Your Life Today With Some of the Greatest Book of 365 Happiness Quotes to Give You the Kickstart You Need!

1

"Time you enjoy wasting is not wasted
time."
— Marthe Troly-Curtin

2

"It's so hard to forget pain, but it's even
harder to remember sweetness. We have no
scar to show for happiness. We learn so little
from peace."
— Chuck Palahniuk

3

"Happiness in intelligent people is the rarest
thing I know."
— Ernest Hemingway

4

"For every minute you are angry you lose
sixty seconds of happiness."
— Ralph Waldo Emerson

5

"Love is that condition in which the
happiness of another person is essential to
your own."
— Robert A. Heinlein,

6

"Folks are usually about as happy as they
make their minds up to be."
— Abraham Lincoln

7

"Happiness is not something ready made. It comes from your own actions."
— Dalai Lama XIV

8

"Count your age by friends, not years. Count your life by smiles, not tears."
— John Lennon

9

"Every man has his secret sorrows which the world knows not; and often times we call a man cold when he is only sad."
— Henry Wadsworth Longfellow

10

"Happiness is when what you think, what you say, and what you do are in harmony."
— Mahatma Gandhi

11

"There's nothing like deep breaths after laughing that hard. Nothing in the world like a sore stomach for the right reasons."
— Stephen Chbosky

12

"You will never be happy if you continue to search for what happiness consists of. You will never live if you are looking for the meaning of life."
— Albert Camus

13

"If more of us valued food and cheer and song above hoarded gold, it would be a merrier world."
— J.R.R. Tolkien

14

"The most important thing is to enjoy your life—to be happy—it's all that matters."
— Audrey Hepburn

15

"Happiness is a warm puppy."
— Charles M. Schulz

16

"You cannot protect yourself from sadness
without protecting yourself from
happiness."
— Jonathan Safran Foer

17

"They say a person needs just three things to
be truly happy in this world: someone to love,
something to do, and something to hope for."
— Tom Bodett

18

"No medicine cures what happiness cannot."
— Gabriel García Márquez

19

"Let us be grateful to the people who make us happy; they are the charming gardeners who make our souls blossom."
— Marcel Proust

20

"You can't be happy unless you're unhappy sometimes"."
— Lauren Oliver

21

"Hope
Smiles from the threshold of the year to come,
Whispering 'it will be happier'..."
— Alfred Tennyson

22

"It isn't what you have or who you are or where you are or what you are doing that makes you happy or unhappy. It is what you think about it."
— Dale Carnegie

23

"Happiness is having a large, loving, caring, close-knit family in another city."
— George Burns

24

"The only way to find true happiness is to risk being completely cut open."
— Chuck Palahniuk

25

"Of all forms of caution, caution in love is perhaps the most fatal to true happiness."
— Bertrand Russell

26

"Sanity and happiness are an impossible combination."
— Mark Twain

27

"Happiness is the consequence of personal effort. You fight for it, strive for it, insist upon it, and sometimes even travel around the world looking for it. You have to participate relentlessly in the manifestations of your own blessings. And once you have achieved a state of happiness, you must never become lax about maintaining it. You must make a mighty effort to keep swimming upward into that happiness forever, to stay afloat on top of it."
— Elizabeth Gilbert

28

"I've got nothing to do today but smile."
— Paul Simon

29

"Success is getting what you want, happiness
is wanting what you get"
— W.P. Kinsella

30

"I felt my lungs inflate with the onrush of
scenery—air, mountains, trees, people. I
thought, "This is what it is to be happy."
— Sylvia Plath,

31

Happiness [is] only real when shared"
— Jon Krakauer

32

"The worst part of success is trying to find
someone who is happy for you."
— Bette Midler

33

"Happiness is holding someone in your arms
and knowing you hold the whole world."
— Orhan Pamuk

34

"Learn to value yourself, which means: fight
for your happiness."
— Ayn Rand

35

"Letting go means to come to the realization
that some people are a part of your history,
but not a part of your destiny."
— Steve Maraboli

36

"It's been my experience that you can nearly
always enjoy things if you make up your
mind firmly that you will."
— L.M. Montgomery

37

"It's like Tolstoy said. Happiness is an allegory, unhappiness a story."
— Haruki Murakami

38

"please believe that things are good with me, and even when they're not, they will be soon enough. And i will always believe the same about you."
— Stephen Chbosky

39

"I'm happy. Which often looks like crazy."
— David Henry Hwang

40

"Cry. Forgive. Learn. Move on. Let your
tears water the seeds of your future
happiness."
— Steve Maraboli

41

"The grand essentials to happiness in this life
are something to do, something to love, and
something to hope for."
— George Washington Burnap,

42

"Let no one ever come to you without leaving
better and happier. Be the living expression
of God's kindness: kindness in your face,
kindness in your eyes, kindness in your
smile."
— Mother Teresa

43

"When the first baby laughed for the first time, its laugh broke into a thousand pieces, and they all went skipping about, and that was the beginning of fairies."
— J.M. Barrie

44

"All happiness depends on courage and work."
— Honoré de Balzac

45

"The best way to cheer yourself is to try to cheer someone else up."
— Mark Twain

46

"I am not proud, but I am happy; and
happiness blinds, I think, more than pride."
— Alexandre Dumas

47

"I think and think and think, I've thought
myself out of happiness one million times, but
never once into it."
— Jonathan Safran Foer

48

"I must learn to be content with being
happier than I deserve."
— Jane Austen

49

"So we shall let the reader answer this question for himself: who is the happier man, he who has braved the storm of life and lived or he who has stayed securely on shore and merely existed?"
— Hunter S. Thompson

50

"Man only likes to count his troubles; he doesn't calculate his happiness."
— Fyodor Dostoyevsky

51

"The advantage of a bad memory is that one enjoys several times the same good things for the first time."
— Friedrich Nietzsche

52

"Happiness quite unshared can scarcely be
called happiness; it has no taste."
— Charlotte Brontë

53

"And hand in hand, on the edge of the sand,
They danced by the light of the moon."
— Edward Lear

54

"One of the keys to happiness is a bad
memory."
— Rita Mae Brown

55

"Happiness depends upon ourselves."
— Aristotle

56

"I know that's what people say-- you'll get over it. I'd say it, too. But I know it's not true. Oh, youll be happy again, never fear. But you won't forget. Every time you fall in love it will be because something in the man reminds you of him."
— Betty Smith

57

"The happiness of your life depends upon the quality of your thoughts."
— Marcus Aurelius

58

"It was only a sunny smile, and little it cost
in the giving, but like morning light it
scattered the night and made the day worth
living."
— F. Scott Fitzgerald

59

"I'd far rather be happy than right any day."
— Douglas Adams

60

"Now and then it's good to pause in our
pursuit of happiness and just be happy."
— Guillaume Apollinaire

61

"People like to say love is unconditional, but it's not, and even if it was unconditional, it's still never free. There's always an expectation attached. They always want something in return. Like they want you to be happy or whatever and that makes you automatically responsible for their happiness because they won't be happy unless you are ... I just don't want that responsibility."
— Katja Millay

62

"Happiness makes up in height for what it lacks in length."
— Robert Frost

63

"If you want to be happy, do not dwell in the past, do not worry about the future, focus on living fully in the present."
— Roy T. Bennett

64

"I felt once more how simple and frugal a thing is happiness: a glass of wine, a roast chestnut, a wretched little brazier, the sound of the sea. Nothing else."
— Nikos Kazantzakis

65

"Happiness is not the absence of problems, it's the ability to deal with them."
— Steve Maraboli

66

"Sometimes life knocks you on your ass... get up, get up, get up!!! Happiness is not the absence of problems, it's the ability to deal with them."
— Steve Maraboli,

67

"Maybe the truth is, there's a little bit of loser in all of us. Being happy isn't having everything in your life be perfect. Maybe it's about stringing together all the little things."
— Ann Brashares

68

"Actual happiness always looks pretty squalid in comparison with the overcompensations for misery. And, of course, stability isn't nearly so spectacular as instability. And being contented has none of the glamour of a good fight against misfortune, none of the picturesqueness of a struggle with temptation, or a fatal overthrow by passion or doubt. Happiness is never grand."
— Aldous Huxley

69

"Happiness is the meaning and the purpose of life, the whole aim and end of human existence."
— Aristotle

70

Happiness is an accident of nature, a beautiful and flawless aberration."
— Pat Conroy

71

"I am the happiest creature in the world. Perhaps other people have said so before, but not one with such justice. I am happier even than Jane; she only smiles, I laugh."
— Jane Austen

72

"Ester asked why people are sad. "That's simple," says the old man. "They are the prisoners of their personal history. Everyone believes that the main aim in life is to follow a plan. They never ask if that plan is theirs or if it was created by another person. They accumulate experiences, memories, things, other people's ideas, and it is more than they can possibly cope with. And that is why they forget their dreams."
— Paulo Coelho

73

"With mirth and laughter let old wrinkles
come."
— William Shakespeare

74

"I do not miss childhood, but I miss the way I
took pleasure in small things, even as greater
things crumbled. I could not control the world
I was in, could not walk away from things or
people or moments that hurt, but I took joy in
the things that made me happy."
— Neil Gaiman

75

"Happily ever after, or even just together
ever after, is not cheesy," Wren said. "It's the
noblest, like, the most courageous thing two
people can shoot for."
— Rainbow Rowell

76

"The secret of happiness is freedom, the secret of freedom is courage."
— Carrie Jones

77

"A quiet secluded life in the country, with the possibility of being useful to people to whom it is easy to do good, and who are not accustomed to have it done to them; then work which one hopes may be of some use; then rest, nature, books, music, love for one's neighbor — such is my idea of happiness."
— Leo Tolstoy

78

"There are two ways to get enough. One is to continue to accumulate more and more. The other is to desire less."
— G.K. Chesterton

79

"Those who are not looking for happiness are the most likely to find it, because those who are searching forget that the surest way to be happy is to seek happiness for others."
— Martin Luther King Jr.

80

"There is nothing more rare, nor more beautiful, than a woman being unapologetically herself; comfortable in her perfect imperfection. To me, that is the true essence of beauty."
— Steve Maraboli

81

"It is the very mark of the spirit of rebellion to crave for happiness in this life"
— Henrik Ibsen, Ghosts

82

"I'm choosing happiness over suffering, I know I am. I'm making space for the unknown future to fill up my life with yet-to-come surprises."
— Elizabeth Gilbert

83

"There is some kind of a sweet innocence in being human- in not having to be just happy or just sad- in the nature of being able to be both broken and whole, at the same time."
— C. JoyBell C.

84

"Whoever is happy will make others happy."
— Anne Frank

85

"A mathematical formula for happiness:Reality divided by Expectations.There were two ways to be happy:improve your reality or lower your expectations."
— Jodi Picoult

86

"This planet has - or rather had - a problem, which was this: most of the people living on it were unhappy for pretty much of the time. Many solutions were suggested for this problem, but most of these were largely concerned with the movement of small green pieces of paper, which was odd because on the whole it wasn't the small green pieces of paper that were unhappy."
— Douglas Adams

87

"I will not try to convince you to love me, to respect me, to commit to me. I deserve better than that; I AM BETTER THAN THAT...Goodbye."
— Steve Maraboli

88

"People are unhappy when they get
something too easily. You have to sweat--
that's the only moral they know."
— Dany Laferrière

89

"I think happiness is what makes you pretty.
Period. Happy people are beautiful. They
become like a mirror and they reflect that
happiness."
— Drew Barrymore

90

"Keep your best wishes, close to your heart
and watch what happens"
— Tony DeLiso

91

"I, not events, have the power to make me happy or unhappy today. I can choose which it shall be. Yesterday is dead, tomorrow hasn't arrived yet. I have just one day, today, and I'm going to be happy in it."
— Groucho Marx

92

"Children are happy because they don't have a file in their minds called "All the Things That Could Go Wrong."
— Marianne Williamson

93

"Laughter is poison to fear."
— George R.R. Martin

94

"I have no faith in human perfectibility. I think that human exertion will have no appreciable effect upon humanity. Man is now only more active - not more happy - nor more wise, than he was 6000 years ago."
— Edgar Allan Poe

95

"Attitude is a choice. Happiness is a choice. Optimism is a choice. Kindness is a choice. Giving is a choice. Respect is a choice. Whatever choice you make makes you. Choose wisely."
— Roy T. Bennett

96

"With all its sham, drudgery, and broken dreams,
it is still a beautiful world.
Be cheerful.
Strive to be happy."
— Max Ehrmann

97

"Happiness is not a goal...it's a by-product of
a life well lived."
— Eleanor Roosevelt

98

"We don't even ask happiness, just a little
less pain."
— Charles Bukowski

99

"I have a million things to talk to you about.
All I want in this world is you. I want to see
you and talk. I want the two of us to begin
everything from the beginning."
— Haruki Murakami

100

"Don't sacrifice yourself too much, because if you sacrifice too much there's nothing else you can give and nobody will care for you."
— Karl Lagerfeld

101

"I don't know what's worse: to not know what you are and be happy, or to become what you've always wanted to be, and feel alone."
— Daniel Keyes

102

"The greater part of our happiness or misery depends upon our dispositions, and not upon our circumstances."
— Martha Washington

103

"That's the difference between me and the rest of the world! Happiness isn't good enough for me! I demand euphoria!"
— Bill Watterson

104

"Happiness is not a possession to be prized, it is a quality of thought, a state of mind."
— Daphne du Maurier

105

"And I can't be running back and fourth forever between grief and high delight."
— J.D. Salinger

106

"I heard a definition once: Happiness is health and a short memory! I wish I'd invented it, because it is very true."
— Audrey Hepburn

107

"A thing of beauty is a joy forever."
— John Keats,

108

"I am very happy
Because I have conquered myself
And not the world.
I am very happy
Because I have loved the world
And not myself."
— Sri Chinmoy

109

"You'll learn, as you get older, that rules are made to be broken. Be bold enough to live life on your terms, and never, ever apologize for it. Go against the grain, refuse to conform, take the road less traveled instead of the well-beaten path. Laugh in the face of adversity, and leap before you look. Dance as though EVERYBODY is watching. March to the beat of your own drummer. And stubbornly refuse to fit in."
— Mandy Hale,

110

"The problem with people is they forget that most of the time it's the small things that count."
— Jennifer Niven

111

"The power of finding beauty in the humblest things makes home happy and life lovely."
— Louisa May Alcott

112

"Letting go gives us freedom, and freedom is the only condition for happiness. If, in our heart, we still cling to anything - anger, anxiety, or possessions - we cannot be free."
— Thich Nhat Hanh

113

"I am a happy camper so I guess I'm doing something right. Happiness is like a butterfly; the more you chase it, the more it will elude you, but if you turn your attention to other things, it will come and sit softly on your shoulder."
— J. Richard Lessor

114

"I am a happy camper so I guess I'm doing something right. Happiness is like a butterfly; the more you chase it, the more it will elude you, but if you turn your attention to other things, it will come and sit softly on your shoulder."
— J. Richard Lessor

115

"The sense of unhappiness is so much easier to convey than that of happiness. In misery we seem aware of our own existence, even though it may be in the form of a monstrous egotism: this pain of mine is individual, this nerve that winces belongs to me and to no other. But happiness annihilates us: we lose our identity."
— Graham Greene

116

"The more you feed your mind with positive thoughts, the more you can attract great things into your life."
— Roy T. Bennett

117

"I find the best way to love someone is not to change them, but instead, help them reveal the greatest version of themselves."
— Steve Maraboli

118

"What can I do with my happiness? How can I keep it, conceal it, bury it where I may never lose it? I want to kneel as it falls over me like rain, gather it up with lace and silk, and press it over myself again."
— Anaïs Nin

119

"Always find opportunities to make someone smile, and to offer random acts of kindness in everyday life."
— Roy T. Bennett

120

"I've always thought people would find a lot more pleasure in their routines if they burst into song at significant moments."
— John Barrowman

121

"Be grateful for what you already have while you pursue your goals.
If you aren't grateful for what you already have, what makes you think you would be happy with more."
— Roy T. Bennett

122

"I'm a kind of paranoiac in reverse. I suspect people of plotting to make me happy."
— J.D. Salinger,

123

"If only we'd stop trying to be happy, we could have a pretty good time."
— Edith Wharton

124

"Stop giving other people the power to control your happiness, your mind, and your life. If you don't take control of yourself and your own life, someone else is bound to try."
— Roy T. Bennett

125

"The pain I feel now is the happiness I had before. That's the deal."
— C.S. Lewis

126

"Happiness is a risk. If you're not a little scared, then you're not doing it right."
— Sarah Addison Allen

127

"This life is yours. Take the power to choose what you want to do and do it well. Take the power to love what you want in life and love it honestly. Take the power to walk in the forest and be a part of nature. Take the power to control your own life. No one else can do it for you. Take the power to make your life happy."
— Susan Polis Schutz

128

"Happiness consists in frequent repetition of pleasure"
— Arthur Schopenhauer

129

"The more you praise and celebrate your life, the more there is in life to celebrate."
— Oprah Winfrey

130

"Happiness. It was the place where passion, with all its dazzle and drumbeat, met something softer: homecoming and safety and pure sunbeam comfort. It was all those things, intertwined with the heat and the thrill, and it was as bright within her as a swallowed star."
— Laini Taylor

131

"Take responsibility of your own happiness, never put it in other people's hands."
— Roy T. Bennett,

132

"Top 15 Things Money Can't Buy
Time. Happiness. Inner Peace. Integrity. Love. Character. Manners. Health. Respect. Morals. Trust. Patience. Class. Common sense. Dignity."
— Roy T. Bennett,

133

"No one should ever ask themselves that: why am I unhappy? The question carries within it the virus that will destroy everything. If we ask that question, it means we want to find out what makes us happy. If what makes us happy is different from what we have now, then we must either change once and for all or stay as we are, feeling even more unhappy."
— Paulo Coelho

134

"Happiness consists in frequent repetition of pleasure"
— Arthur Schopenhauer

135

"The more you praise and celebrate your life, the more there is in life to celebrate."
— Oprah Winfrey

136

"My happiness is not the means to any end. It is the end. It is its own goal. It is its own purpose."
— Ayn Rand

137

"All who joy would win
Must share it -- Happiness was born a twin."
— George Gordon Byron

138

"Wealth consists not in having great possessions, but in having few wants."
— Epictetus

139

"It does not matter how long you are spending on the earth, how much money you have gathered or how much attention you have received. It is the amount of positive vibration you have radiated in life that matters,"
— Amit Ray

140

"Life is not a PG feel-good movie. Real life often ends badly. Literature tries to document this reality, while showing us it is still possible for us to endure nobly."
— Matthew Quick

141

"I had rather hear my dog bark at a crow, than a man swear he loves me."
— William Shakespeare

142

"Even if things don't unfold the way you expected, don't be disheartened or give up. One who continues to advance will win in the end."
— Daisaku Ikeda

143

"If you want others to be happy, practice compassion. If you want to be happy, practice compassion."
— Dalai Lama XIV

144

"There is no happiness like that of being loved by your fellow creatures, and feeling that your presence is an addition to their comfort."
— Charlotte Brontë

145

"We all live with the objective of being happy; our lives are all different and yet the same."
— Anne Frank

146

"Perfectionism is the enemy of happiness. Embrace being perfectly imperfect. Learn from your mistakes and forgive yourself, you'll be happier. We make mistakes because we are imperfect. Learn from your mistakes, forgive yourself, and keep moving forward."
— Roy T. Bennett

147

"It takes three to make love, not two: you, your spouse, and God. Without God people only succeed in bringing out the worst in one another. Lovers who have nothing else to do but love each other soon find there is nothing else. Without a central loyalty life is unfinished."
— Fulton J. Sheen

148

"Be believing, be happy, don't get discouraged. Things will work out."
— Gordon B. Hinckley

149

"The belief that unhappiness is selfless and happiness is selfish is misguided. It's more selfless to act happy. It takes energy, generosity, and discipline to be unfailingly lighthearted, yet everyone takes the happy person for granted. No one is careful of his feelings or tries to keep his spirits high. He seems self-sufficient; he becomes a cushion for others. And because happiness seems unforced, that person usually gets no credit."
— Gretchen Rubin,

150

"those who do not know how to see the precious things in life will never be happy."
— Alex Flinn

151

"Very little is needed to make a happy life; it
is all within yourself in your way of
thinking."
— Marcus Aurelius

152

"Happiness. Simple as a glass of chocolate or
tortuous as the heart. Bitter. Sweet. Alive."
— Joanne Harris

153

"All I ask is one thing, and I'm asking this
particularly of young people: please don't be
cynical. I hate cynicism, for the record, it's
my least favorite quality and it doesn't lead
anywhere. Nobody in life gets exactly what
they thought they were going to get. But if
you work really hard and you're kind,
amazing things will happen."
— Conan O'Brien

154

"Happy girls are the prettiest"
— Audrey Hepburn

155

"There you go...let it all slide out.
Unhappiness can't stick in a person's soul
when it's slick with tears."
— Shannon Hale,

156

"And therein lies the whole of man's plight.
Human time does not turn in a circle; it runs
ahead in a straight line. That is why man
cannot be happy: happiness is the longing for
repetition."
— Milan Kundera

157

"Success is getting what you want..
Happiness is wanting what you get."
— Dale Carnegie

158

"It is sometimes easier to be happy if you don't
know everything."
— Alexander McCall Smith

159

"The only time you fail is when you fall down
and stay down."
— Stephen Richards

160

"They've got no idea what happiness is, they don't know that without this love there is no happiness or unhappiness for us--there is no life."
— Leo Tolstoy

161

"Happiness is a perfume you cannot pour on others without getting some on yourself."
— Ralph Waldo Emerson

162

"Plant seeds of happiness, hope, success, and love; it will all come back to you in abundance. This is the law of nature."
— Steve Maraboli

163

"Love is too precious to be ashamed of."
— Laurell K. Hamilton

164

"Just because you are happy it does not mean
that the day is perfect but that you have
looked beyond its imperfections"
— Bob Marley

165

"We buy things we don't need with money we
don't have to impress people we don't like."
— Dave Ramsey

166

"I don't think that there are any limits to how excellent we could make life seem."
— Jonathan Safran Foer

167

"You cannot be with someone just because you don't want to hurt him. You have your own happiness to think about."
— Melissa de la Cruz

168

"I am intrigued by the smile upon your face, and the sadness within your eyes"
— Jeremy Aldana

169

"Let us dance in the sun, wearing wild
flowers in our hair..."
— Susan Polis Schutz

170

"Sometimes you break your heart in the right
way, if you know what I mean."
— Gregory David Roberts

171

"You can't be brave if you've only had
wonderful things happen to you."
— Mary Tyler Moore

172

"Don't waste your time in anger, regrets, worries, and grudges. Life is too short to be unhappy."
— Roy T. Bennett

173

"My past has not defined me, destroyed me, deterred me, or defeated me; it has only strengthened me."
— Steve Maraboli,

174

"Woman is not made to be the admiration of all, but the happiness of one."
— Edmund Burke

175

"We're all golden sunflowers inside."
— Allen Ginsberg

176

"The trick is in what one emphasizes. We either make ourselves miserable, or we make ourselves happy. The amount of work is the same."
— Carlos Castaneda

177

"Memory is the happiness of being alone."
— Lois Lowry

178

"Stop comparing yourself to other people, just choose to be happy and live your own life."
— Roy T. Bennett

179

"Feathers filled the small room. Our laughter kept the feathers in the air. I thought about birds. Could they fly if there wasn't someone, somewhere, laughing?"
— Jonathan Safran Foer

180

"Only the development of compassion and understanding for others can bring us the tranquility and happiness we all seek."
— Dalai Lama XIV

181

"Happiness was but the occasional episode
in a general drama of pain."
— Thomas Hardy

182

"There is only one way to happiness and that
is to cease worrying about things which are
beyond the power or our will. "
— Epictetus

183

"Obscurity and a competence—that is the
life that is best worth living."
— Mark Twain,

184

"Happiness was but the occasional episode
in a general drama of pain."
— Thomas Hardy

185

"People wait around too long for love. I'm
happy with all of my lusts!"
— C. JoyBell C.

186

"Happy. Just in my swim shorts, barefooted,
wild-haired, in the red fire dark, singing,
swigging wine, spitting, jumping, running
—that's the way to live. All alone and free in
the soft sands of the beach by the sigh of the
sea out there, with the Ma-Wink fallopian
virgin warm stars reflecting on the outer
channel fluid belly waters. And if your cans
are redhot and you can't hold them in your
hands, just use good old railroad gloves,
that's all."
— Jack Kerouac

187

"Money may not buy happiness, but I'd rather cry in a Jaguar than on a bus."
— Françoise Sagan

188

"You have to participate relentlessly in the manifestation of your own blessings."
— Elizabeth Gilbert

189

"There are two ways to be happy: improve your reality, or lower your expectations."
— Jodi Picoult

190

"But maybe happiness isn't in the choosing. Maybe it's in the fiction, in the pretending: that wherever we have ended up is where we intended to be all along."
— Lauren Oliver

191

"Expectations make people miserable, so whatever yours are, lower them. You'll definitely be happier."
— Simone Elkeles

192

"Pierre was right when he said that one must believe in the possibility of happiness in order to be happy, and I now believe in it. Let the dead bury the dead, but while I'm alive, I must live and be happy."
— Leo Tolstoy

193

"Later she remembered all the hours of the afternoon as happy -- one of those uneventful times that seem at the moment only a link between past and future pleasure, but turn out to have been the pleasure itself."
— F. Scott Fitzgerald

194

"People tend to think that happiness is a stroke of luck, something that will descend like fine weather if you're fortunate. But happiness is the result of personal effort. You fight for it, strive for it, insist upon it, and sometimes even travel around the world looking for it. You have to participate relentlessly."
— Elizabeth Gilbert

195

"Happiness doesn't result from what we get, but from what we give."
— Ben Carson

196

"Many people think excitement is happiness.... But when you are excited you are not peaceful. True happiness is based on peace."
— Thich Nhat Hanh

197

"It's a helluva start, being able to recognize what makes you happy. "
— Lucille Ball

198

"Smile more. Smiling can make you and others happy."
— Roy T. Bennett

199

"Humanity does not ask us to be happy. It merely asks us to be brilliant on its behalf."
— Orson Scott Card

200

"Art is unquestionably one of the purest and highest elements in human happiness. It trains the mind through the eye, and the eye through the mind. As the sun colors flowers, so does art color life."
— John Lubbock

201

"One swallow does not make a summer, neither does one fine day; similarly one day or brief time of happiness does not make a person entirely happy."
— Aristotle

202

"Do not set aside your happiness. Do not wait to be happy in the future. The best time to be happy is always now."
— Roy T. Bennett

203

"Is anyone anywhere happy?"
— Sylvia Plath

204

"It is difficult to live in and enjoy the moment when you are thinking about the past or worrying about the future. You cannot change your past, but you can ruin the present by worrying about your future. Learn from the past, plan for the future. The more you live in and enjoy the present moment, the happier you will be."
— Roy T. Bennett

205

"I don't understand the point of being together if you're not the happiest."
— Gillian Flynn

206

"Ever since happiness heard your name, it has been running through the streets trying to find you."
— Hafez

207

"Even if you cannot change all the people around you, you can change the people you choose to be around. Life is too short to waste your time on people who don't respect, appreciate, and value you. Spend your life with people who make you smile, laugh, and feel loved."
— Roy T. Bennett

208

"Happiness is not achieved by the conscious pursuit of happiness; it is generally the by-product of other activities."
— Aldous Huxley

209

"There is no beauty in sadness. No honor in suffering. No growth in fear. No relief in hate. It's just a waste of perfectly good happiness."
— Katerina Stoykova Klemer

210

"My God, a moment of bliss. Why, isn't that enough for a whole lifetime?"
— Fyodor Dostoyevsky

211

"If you have any young friends who aspire to become writers, the second greatest favor you can do them is to present them with copies of The Elements of Style. The first greatest, of course, is to shoot them now, while they're happy."
— Dorothy Parker

212

"it is impossible to build one's own happiness on the unhappiness of others. This perspective is at the heart of Buddhist teachings."
— Daisaku Ikeda

213

"Always forgive, but never forget, else you will be a prisoner of your own hatred, and doomed to repeat your mistakes forever."
— Wil Zeus

214

"It is a happiness to wonder; -- it is a
happiness to dream."
— Edgar Allan Poe

215

"Singing in the rain. I'm singing in the rain.
And it's such a fucking glorious feeling. An
unexpected downpour and I am just giving
myself into it. Because what the fuck else can
you do? Run for cover? Shriek and curse? No--
when the rain falls you just let it fall and you
grin like a madman and you dance with it
because if you can make yourself happy in the
rain, then you're doing pretty alright in life."
— David Levithan

216

"The present moment is filled with joy and
happiness. If you are attentive, you will see
it. (21)"
— Thich Nhat Hanh

217

"To be stupid, and selfish, and to have good health are the three requirements for happiness - though if stupidity is lacking, the others are useless."
— Julian Barnes

218

"Seize the moments of happiness, love and be loved! That is the only reality in the world, all else is folly. It is the one thing we are interested in here."
— Leo Tolstoy

219

"Everyone wants to live on top of the mountain, but all the happiness and growth occurs while you're climbing it."
— Andy Rooney

220

"right in this moment, I can´t even
remember what unhappy feels like."
— Maggie Stiefvater

221

"right in this moment, I can´t even remember
what unhappy feels like."
— Maggie Stiefvater

222

"The true measure of success is how many
times you can bounce back from failure."
— Stephen Richards

223

"[F]or just one second, look at your life and see how perfect it is. Stop looking for the next secret door that is going to lead you to your real life. Stop waiting. This is it: there's nothing else. It's here, and you'd better decide to enjoy it or you're going to be miserable wherever you go, for the rest of your life, forever."
— Lev Grossman,

224

"Happiness depends on your mindset and attitude."
— Roy T. Bennett

225

"When you connect to the silence within you, that is when you can make sense of the disturbance going on around you."
— Stephen Richards

226

"The secret of happiness is not in doing what one likes, but in liking what one does."
— J.M. Barrie

227

"What sunshine is to flowers, smiles are to humanity. These are but trifles, to be sure; but scattered along life's pathway, the good they do is inconceivable."
— Joseph Addison

228

"There are random moments - tossing a salad, coming up the driveway to the house, ironing the seams flat on a quilt square, standing at the kitchen window and looking out at the delphiniums, hearing a burst of laughter from one of my children's rooms - when I feel a wavelike rush of joy. This is my true religion: arbitrary moments of of nearly painful happiness for a life I feel privileged to lead."
— Elizabeth Berg,

229

"Everybody in the world is seeking happiness
—and there is one sure way to find it. That is
by controlling your thoughts. Happiness
doesn't depend on outward conditions. It
depends on inner conditions."
— Dale Carnegie

230

"Nothing makes a person happier than having
a happy heart."
— Roy T. Bennett

231

"Until you make peace with who you are,
you'll never be content with what you have."
— Doris Mortman

232

"Happiness depends on being free, and freedom depends on being courageous."
— Marie Rutkoski

233

"You, of all people, deserve a happy ending. Despite everything that happened to you, you aren't bitter. You aren't cold. You've just retreated a little and been shy, and that's okay. If I were a fairy godmother, I would give you your heart's desire in an istant. And I would wipe away your tears and tell you not to cry.

-Rachel to Julia"
— Sylvain Reynard

234

"Can a person steal happiness? Or is just another internal, infernal human trick?"
— Markus Zusak

235

"You don't ask people with knives in their stomachs what would make them happy; happiness is no longer the point. It's all about survival; it's all about whether you pull the knife out and bleed to death or keep it in..."
— Nick Hornby

236

"Growing old is mandatory. Growing up is optional."
— Carroll Bryant

237

"So he tasted the deep pain that is reserved only for the strong, just as he had tasted for a little while the deep happiness."
— F. Scott Fitzgerald

238

"The foolish man seeks happiness in the distance. The wise grows it under his feet."
— James Oppenheim

239

"There is a kind of happiness and wonder that makes you serious. It is too good to waste on jokes."
— C.S. Lewis

240

"Destiny is real. And she's not mild-mannered. She will come around and hit you in the face and knock you over and before you know what hit you, you're naked-stripped of everything you thought you knew and everything you thought you didn't know-and there you are! A bloody nose, bruises all over you, and naked. And it's the most beautiful thing."
— C. JoyBell C.

241

"I am not good at noticing when I'm happy,
except in retrospect."
— Tana French

242

"Ahhh. Bed, book, kitten, sandwich. All one
needed in life, really."
— Jacqueline Kelly

243

"Happiness doesn't lie in conspicuous
consumption and the relentless amassing of
useless crap. Happiness lies in the person
sitting beside you and your ability to talk to
them. Happiness is clear-headed human
interaction and empathy. Happiness is home.
And home is not a house-home is a
mythological conceit. It is a state of mind. A
place of communion and unconditional love.
It is where, when you cross its threshold, you
finally feel at peace."
— Dennis Lehane

244

"The reason people find it so hard to be happy is that they always see the past better than it was, the present worse than it is, and the future less resolved than it will be."
— Marcel Pagnol

245

"That's life for you. All the happiness you gather to yourself, it will sweep away like it's nothing. If you ask me I don't think there are any such things as curses. I think there is only life. That's enough."
— Junot Díaz

246

"The trouble is that we have a bad habit, encouraged by pedants and sophisticates, of considering happiness as something rather stupid. Only pain is intellectual, only evil interesting. This is the treason of the artist; a refusal to admit the banality of evil and the terrible boredom of pain."
— Ursula K. Le Guin,

247

"And I didn't choose it, Kat. I chose you."
— Ally Carter

248

"I believe compassion to be one of the few things we can practice that will bring immediate and long-term happiness to our lives. I'm not talking about the short-term gratification of pleasures like sex, drugs or gambling (though I'm not knocking them), but something that will bring true and lasting happiness. The kind that sticks."
— Dalai Lama XIV

249

"Happiness only real when shared."
— Christopher McCandless

250

"You must be the best judge of your own happiness."
— Jane Austen

251

"Life is painful. It has thorns, like the stem of a rose. Culture and art are the roses that bloom on the stem. The flower is yourself, your humanity. Art is the liberation of the humanity inside yourself."
— Daisaku Ikeda

252

"Puritanism: The haunting fear that someone, somewhere, may be happy."
— H.L. Mencken

253

"Perfect love casts out fear. Where there is love there are no demands, no expectations, no dependency. I do not demand that you make me happy; my happiness does not lie in you. If you were to leave me, I will not feel sorry for myself; I enjoy your company immensely, but I do not cling."
— Anthony de Mello

254

"One is happy as a result of one's own efforts once one knows the necessary ingredients of happiness: simple tastes, a certain degree of courage, self denial to a point, love of work, and above all, a clear conscience."
— George Sand

255

"When you are joyful, when you say yes to life and have fun and project positivity all around you, you become a sun in the center of every constellation, and people want to be near you."
— Shannon L. Alder

256

"Happiness is part of who we are. Joy is the feeling"
— Tony DeLiso

257

"I shall take the heart. For brains do not make one happy, and happiness is the best thing in the world.
"

— L. Frank Baum

258

"You are in charge of your own happiness; you don't need to wait for other people's permission to be happy."
— Roy T. Bennett

259

"Happiness is the most natural thing in the world when you have it, and the slowest, strangest, most impossible thing when you don't. It's like learning a foreign language: You can think about the words all you want, but you'll never be able to speak it until you suck up your courage and say them out loud."
— Dan Wells

260

"It isn't what you have, or who you are, or where you are, or what you are doing that makes you happy or unhappy. It is what you think about."
— Dale Carnegie

261

"If you wish to be happy,Eragon, Think not of what is to come nor of that which you have no control over but rather of the now and that which you are able to change" ~Oromis to eragon ,Brisingr~618"
— Christopher Paolini

262

"My happiness grows in direct proportion to my acceptance, and in inverse proportion to my expectations."
— Michael J. Fox

263

"My only regrets are the moments when i doubted myself and took the safe route. Life is too short to waste time being unhappy."
— Dan Howell

264

"Having a low opinion of yourself is not 'modesty.' It's self-destruction. Holding your uniqueness in high regard is not 'egotism.' It's a necessary precondition to happiness and success."
— Bobbe Sommer

265

"You can't buy happiness"
— Kurt Cobain

266

"I don't know what your destiny will be, but one thing I know: the only ones among you who will be really happy are those who have sought and found how to serve."
— Albert Schweitzer

267

"She had never imagined she had the power to make someone else so happy. And not a magical power, either--a purely human one."
— Cassandra Clare

268

"dear today,

i spend all of you pretending i'm okay when i'm not, pretending i'm happy when i'm not, pretending about everything to everyone."
— Nina LaCour,

269

"Happiness and the absurd are two sons of the same earth. They are inseparable."
— Albert Camus

270

"You have everything you need for complete peace and total happiness right now."
— Wayne W. Dyer

271

"That's how stories happen — with a turning point, an unexpected twist. There's only one kind of happiness, but misfortune comes in all shapes and sizes. It's like Tolstoy said. Happiness is an allegory, unhappiness a story."
— Haruki Murakami,

272

"Dustfinger still clearly remembered the feeling of being in love for the first time. How vulnerable his heart had suddenly been! Such a trembling, quivering thing, happy and miserably unhappy at once."
— Cornelia Funke

273

"Those born to wealth, and who have the means of gratifying every wish, know not what is the real happiness of life, just as those who have been tossed on the stormy waters of the ocean on a few frail planks can alone realize the blessings of fair weather."
— Alexandre Dumas

274

"Happiness, you see, its just an illusion of Fate, a heavenly sleight of hand designed to make you believe in fairy tales. But there's no happily ever after. You'll only find happy endings in books. Some books."
— Ellen Hopkins

275

"Happiness comes from within. It is not dependent on external things or on other people. You become vulnerable and can be easily hurt when your feelings of security and happiness depend on the behavior and actions of other people. Never give your power to anyone else."
— Brian L. Weiss

276

"A large income is the best recipe for happiness I ever heard of."
— Jane Austen

277

"Happiness is excitement that has found a settling down place, but there is always a little corner that keeps flapping around."
— E.L. Konigsburg

278

"I may never be happy, but tonight I am content."
— Sylvia Plath

279

"Changing your outside world cannot make you happy if you are an unhappy person. The real personal change can only happen from the inside out. If you firstly create the change within yourself, you can turn your life around."
— Roy T. Bennett,

280

"If you've got nothing to dance about, find a
reason to sing."
— Melody Carstairs

281

"I think, that if the world were a bit more like
ComicCon, it would be a better place."
— Matt Smith

282

"With my eyes closed, I would touch a
familiar book and draw its fragrance deep
inside me. This was enough to make me
happy. "
— Haruki Murakami

283

"Really high-minded people are indifferent
to happiness, especially other people's."
— Bertrand Russell

284

"It is almost as if happiness is an acquired
taste, like coconut cordial or ceviche, to
which you can eventually become
accustomed, but despair is something
surprising each time you encounter it."
— Lemony Snicket

285

"Most people would rather be certain they're
miserable, than risk being happy."
— Robert Anthony

286

"Freedom is the only worthy goal in life. It is won by disregarding things that lie beyond our control."
— Epictetus

287

"Laugh, and the world laughs with you;
Weep, and you weep alone;
For the sad old earth must borrow its mirth,
But has trouble enough of its own."
— Ella Wheeler Wilcox

288

"Love yourself. Forgive yourself. Be true to yourself. How you treat yourself sets the standard for how others will treat you."
— Steve Maraboli, Unapologetically You: Reflections on Life and the Human Experience

289

"Hurt is a part of life. To be honest, I think hurt is a part of happiness, that our definition of happiness has gotten very narrow lately, very nervous, a little afraid of this brawling, fabulous, unpredictable world."
— Julian Gough

290

"Age does not make us childish, as some say; it finds us true children."
— Johann Wolfgang von Goethe

291

"If you are not the hero of your own story, then you're missing the whole point of your humanity."
— Steve Maraboli

292

"Happiness is a choice that requires effort at times."
— Aeschylus

293

"Exactly. How can you know it makes you happy if you've never experienced it?"
"There are different kinds of happy," she said.
"Some kinds don't need any proof."
— Jennifer E. Smith

294

"Sometimes we must undergo hardships, breakups, and narcissistic wounds, which shatter the flattering image that we had of ourselves, in order to discover two truths: that we are not who we thought we were; and that the loss of a cherished pleasure is not necessarily the loss of true happiness and well-being. (109)"
— Jean-Yves Leloup

295

"He whose face gives no light, shall never
become a star."
— William Blake

296

"I do not think we have a "right" to happiness.
If happiness happens, say thanks."
— Marlene Dietrich

297

"The secret of happiness is to face the fact
that the world is horrible, horrible, horrible."
— Bertrand Russell

298

"Of all the means to insure happiness throughout the whole life, by far the most important is the acquisition of friends."
— Epicurus

299

"Laughter is more than just a pleasurable activity...When people laugh together, they tend to talk and touch more and to make eye contact more frequently."
— Gretchen Rubin

300

"We have to go. I'm almost happy here."
— Orson Scott Card

301

"To serve is beautiful, but only if it is done with joy and a whole heart and a free mind."
— Pearl S. Buck

302

"I'm going to enjoy every second, and I'm going to know I'm enjoying it while I'm enjoying it. Most people don't live; they just race. They are trying to reach some goal far away on the horizon, and in the heat of the going they get so breathless and panting that they lose sight of the beautiful, tranquil country they are passing through; and then the first thing they know, they are old and worn out, and it doesn't make any difference whether they've reached the goal or not."
— Jean Webster

303

"Judgment is a negative frequency."
— Stephen Richards

304

"You have a unique gift to offer this world. Be true to yourself, be kind to yourself, read and learn about everything that interests you and keep away from people who bring you down. When you treat yourself kindly and respect the uniqueness of those around you, you will be giving this world an amazing gift... YOU!"
— Steve Maraboli

305

"That's the secret to life... replace one worry with another...."
— Charles M. Schulz

306

"When your back is to the wall and you are facing fear head on, the only way is forward and through it."
— Stephen Richards

307

"When you lose your smile, you lose your
way in the chaos of life."
— Roy T. Bennett

308

"Life is at its best when everything has fallen
out of place, and you decide that you're going
to fight to get them right, not when
everything is going your way and everyone is
praising you."
— Thisuri Wanniarachchi

309

"Come clean with a child heart
Laugh as peaches in the summer wind
Let rain on a house roof be a song
Let the writing on your face
be a smell of apple orchards on late June."
— Carl Sandburg,

310

"Do not look for happiness outside yourself.
The awakened seek happiness inside."
— Petar Dunov

311

Remember, happiness doesn't depend upon
who you are or what you have, it depends
solely upon what you think."
— Dale Carnegie

312

"A lot of the conflict you have in your life
exists simply because you're not living in
alignment; you're not be being true to
yourself."
— Steve Maraboli

313

"Happiness, like unhappiness, is a proactive choice."
— Stephen R. Covey

314

"That is happiness; to be dissolved into something complete and great. When it comes to one, it comes as naturally as sleep."
— Willa Cather

315

"When you are living the best version of yourself, you inspire others to live the best versions of themselves."
— Steve Maraboli

316

"Why not seize the pleasure at once? -- How often is happiness destroyed by preparation, foolish preparation!"
— Jane Austen

317

"Happiness does not come from without, it comes from within"
— Helen Keller

318

"Happiness is the object and design of our existence; and will be the end thereof, if we pursue the path that leads to it; and this path is virtue, uprightness, faithfulness, holiness, and keeping all the commandments of God."
— Joseph Smith Jr.

319

"Happiness lies in the joy of achievement
and the thrill of creative effort."
— Franklin D. Roosevelt

320

"She had been proud of his decision to serve
his country, her heart bursting with love and
admiration the first time she saw him
outfitted in his dress blues. "
— Nicholas Sparks

321

"It was their secret, a secret meant for just
the two of them, and she'd never been able to
imagine how it would sound coming from
someone else. But, somehow, Logan made it
sound just right."
— Nicholas Sparks

322

"Beauty is the purest feeling of the soul.
Beauty arises when soul is satisfied."
— Amit Ray

323

"Ink runs from the corners of my mouth.
There is no happiness like mine.
I have been eating poetry."
— Mark Strand,

324

"Anne was always glad in the happiness of
her friends; but it is sometimes a little lonely
to be surrounded everywhere by happiness
that is not your own."
— L.M. Montgomery

325

"Got no checkbooks, got no banks. Still I'd like to express my thanks - I've got the sun in the mornin' and the moon at night."
— Irving Berlin

326

"Happiness is not a life without pain, but rather a life in which the pain is traded for a worthy price."
— Orson Scott Card

327

"The victim mindset dilutes the human potential. By not accepting personal responsibility for our circumstances, we greatly reduce our power to change them."
— Steve Maraboli

328

"Why should we build our happiness on the opinons of others, when we can find it in our own hearts?"
— Jean-Jacques Rousseau

329

"I think the saddest people always try their hardest to make people happy because they know what it's like to feel absolutely worthless and they don't want anyone else to feel like that."
— Robin Williams

330

"A flower blossoms for its own joy."
— Oscar Wilde

331

"You see, there are some people that one loves, and others that perhaps one would rather be with."
— Henrik Ibsen

332

"The hardest thing about depression is that it is addictive. It begins to feel uncomfortable not to be depressed. You feel guilty for feeling happy."
— Pete Wentz

333

"Create all the happiness you are able to create; remove all the misery you are able to remove. Every day will allow you, --will invite you to add something to the pleasure of others, --or to diminish something of their pains."
— Jeremy Bentham

334

"Everybody has something, that one thing they must do to feel happy. I think this is yours, and I want you to be happy. You don't have to do it, but it's here if you choose to come back to it."
— Ilona Andrews

335

"Happiness is your nature. It is not wrong to desire it. What is wrong is seeking it outside when it is inside."
— Ramana Maharshi

336

"Every time I thought I was being rejected from something good, I was actually being re-directed to something better."
— Steve Maraboli, Unapologetically You: Reflections on Life and the Human Experience

337

"Happiness is a state of mind, a choice, a way of living; it is not something to be achieved, it is something to be experienced."
— Steve Maraboli

338

"It is a kind of spiritual snobbery that makes people think they can be happy without money."
— Albert Camus

339

"The strength of a man isn't seen in the power of his arms. It's seen in the love with which he EMBRACES you."
— Steve Maraboli

340

"You know, people ask me. They say 'Dan, three years later do you really want to be drawing cat whiskers on your face?' but they don't understand. The cat whiskers, they come from within."
— Dan Howell

341

"Joy came always after pain."
— Guillaume Apollinaire

342

"Well, I always know what I want. And when you know what you want--you go toward it. Sometimes you go very fast, and sometimes only an inch a year. Perhaps you feel happier when you go fast. I don't know. I've forgotten the difference long ago, because it really doesn't matter, so long as you move."
— Ayn Rand

343

"Happiness is like those palaces in fairytales whose gates are guarded by dragons: We must fight in order to conquer it."
— Alexandre Dumas

344

"The way I define happiness is being the creator of your experience, choosing to take pleasure in what you have, right now, regardless of the circumstances, while being the best you that you can be."
— Leo Babauta

345

"Some day you will find out that there is far more happiness in another's happiness than in your own."
— Honoré de Balzac

346

"A happy person is not a person in a certain set of circumstances, but rather a person with a certain set of attitudes."
— Hugh Downs

347

"I am still determined to be cheerful and happy, in whatever situation I may be; for I have also learned from experience that the greater part of our happiness or misery depends upon our dispositions, and not upon our circumstances. a"
— Martha Washington

348

"...is ignorance bliss, I don't know, but it's so painful to think, and tell me, what did thinking ever do for me, to what great place did thinking ever bring me? I think and think and think, I've thought myself out of happiness one million times, but never once into it."
— Jonathan Safran Foer

349

"The trick. . .is to find the balance between the bright colors of humor and the serious issues of identity, self-loathing, and the possibility for intimacy and love when it seems no longer possible or, sadder yet, no longer necessary."
— Wendy Wasserstein

350

"The discovery of a new dish does more for the happiness of the human race than the discovery of a star."
— Jean Anthelme Brillat-Savarin,

351

"Her happiness floated like waves of ocean along the coast of her life. She found lyrics of her life in his arms but she never sung her song."
— Santosh Kalwar

352

"Nothing is miserable unless you think it so;
and on the other hand, nothing brings
happiness unless you are content with it."
— Boethius

353

"[I]t is well to have as many holds upon
happiness as possible."
— Jane Austen

354

"They say all marriages are made in heaven,
but so are thunder and lightning."
— Clint Eastwood

355

"Mara, that's the life I want to give you. That's what I'm offering you. I want to fill you life with color and warmth. I want to fill it with light. Give me a chance"
— Francine Rivers

356

"Happiness and confidence are the prettiest things you can wear"
— Taylor Swift

357

"Paradise was always over there, a day's sail away. But it's a funny thing, escapism. You can go far and wide and you can keep moving on and on through places and years, but you never escape your own life. I, finally, knew where my life belonged. Home."
— J. Maarten Troost,

358

"The big reason why folks leave a small town,' Rant used to say, 'is so they can moon over the idea of going back. And the reason they stay put is so they can moon about getting out.'
Rant meant that no one is happy, anywhere."
— Chuck Palahniuk

359

"Happiness wasn't a mystical place to be reached or won--some bright terrain beyond the boundary of misery, a paradise waiting for them to find it--but something to carry doggedly with you through everything, as humble and ordinary as your gear and supplies."
— Laini Taylor

360

"For who would dare to assert that eternal happiness can compensate for a single moment's human suffering"
— Albert Camus

361

"Always be like a water. Float in the times of pain or dance like waves along the wind which touches its surface."
— Santosh Kalwar

362

"Personally I am very pessimistic. But when, for instance, one of my staff has a baby you can't help but bless them for a good future. Because I can't tell that child, 'Oh, you shouldn't have come into this life.' And yet I know the world is heading in a bad direction. So with those conflicting thoughts in mind, I think about what kind of films I should be making."
— Hayao Miyazaki

363

"The summit of happiness is reached when a person is ready to be what he is."
— Desiderius Erasmus

364

"Frugality is one of the most beautiful and joyful words in the English language, and yet one that we are culturally cut off from understanding and enjoying. The consumption society has made us feel that happiness lies in having things, and has failed to teach us the happiness of not having things."
— Elise Boulding

365

"Compassion is the signature of Higher Consciousness. Non-violence is the tool to evolve into the Higher Consciousness."
— Amit Ray

366

"Take all that you can of this book upon reason, and the balance on faith, and you will live and die a happier man. (When a skeptic expressed surprise to see him reading a Bible)"
— Abraham Lincoln